The Quest
for Prayer

The Quest for Prayer

Coming Home to Spirit

Mary-Alice & Richard Jafolla

UNITY® Books

Unity Village, Missouri

First Edition 1999

Copyright © 1999 by Mary-Alice and Richard Jafolla. All rights reserved. No part of this book may be used or reproduced in any manner whatsoever without written permission from Unity School of Christianity except in the case of brief quotations embodied in critical articles and reviews or in the newsletters and lesson plans of licensed Unity teachers and ministers. For information, address Unity Books, Publishers, Unity School of Christianity, 1901 NW Blue Parkway, Unity Village, MO 64065-0001.

Published by the Unity Movement Advisory Council, a joint committee of the Association of Unity Churches and Unity School of Christianity.

To receive a catalog of all Unity publications (books, cassettes, compact discs, and magazines) or to place an order, call the Customer Service Department: (816) 969-2069 or 1-800-669-0282.

Bible quotations are from the Revised Standard Version unless otherwise noted.

Cover design by Melody Burns

Cover photo © Bill Frymire/Masterfile

Interior design by Coleridge Design

Library of Congress Cataloging-in-Publication Data

Jafolla, Mary-Alice.
    The quest for prayer : coming home to spirit / by Mary-Alice & Richard Jafolla. — 1st ed.
        p.   cm.
    Includes bibliographical references.
    ISBN 0-87159-241-X (pbk.)
    1. Prayer—Unity School of Christianity.   I. Jafolla, Richard.
II. Title.
BX9890.U505J343   1999
248.3'2—dc21   99-19763
                                                              CIP

Canada BN 13252 9033 RT

Publisher's Note

The books in this series continue the work started by *The Quest* and *Adventures on the Quest* by Mary-Alice and Richard Jafolla. *The Quest* succeeded in fulfilling its original objectives by effectively presenting an overview of Unity philosophical perspectives and basic beliefs. It also provided Unity churches and centers a vehicle for individual spiritual growth as well as supported community-building by encouraging intergenerational sharing and personal bonding. *The Quest* offered a planned, yearlong exercise in commitment, instruction, and focused learning.

While *The Quest* remains viable in its original form, this new series of books intends a more advanced application of its concept. This series offers a more topic-specific focus and a small-book format adaptable to a shorter course of instruction. This series assumes a basic familiarity with *The Quest* teachings.

All the books in this series are endorsed by the Unity Movement Advisory Council, a joint committee of the Association of Unity Churches and Unity School of Christianity.

Table of Contents

As long as you believe that God is only
   in heaven and does not fill the
   earth—let your words be few.
Only when you come to know
   that you too contain His presence—
   only then can you begin to pray.

                    —Hasidic prayer[1]

Foreword

Dear Friend, this is not *the complete* book on prayer. That one is within your own heart, waiting to be read. These pages are meant only to provide you with a few ideas—a few insights—which may possibly be the catalyst that helps you access your own "book." Hopefully, they will allow you to feel your value as a link in the golden chain of prayer that is encircling our world today.

Our love and blessings to you,
Mary-Alice & Richard Jafolla

Content is a word unknown to life . . . .
Life reaching out, groping for a
billion years, life desperate to go
home.

—Loren Eiseley[2]

Introduction

The journey of the Creator has been an immense one—so long, so winding, so ofttimes obscured in the mists of the past that to this day it still remains untracked. Yet so unrelentingly purposeful has been the mission of this journey that it has never wavered in its quest.

What is this quest of the Creator? Just as humanity has always harbored an insatiable quest to experience the presence of a Supreme Being, the Creator harbors an insatiable quest to experience Itself! Its entire journey has been a cosmic quest to satisfy this hunger. And because the only way the Creator *can* experience Itself is through Its creations, we can understand the eternal drive to create the consummate creature.

With the dawn of Homo sapiens, a creature stepped forth who could acknowledge the existence of its creator. From one tiny cell, each of us develops into a complex masterpiece of creation, aware of itself . . . asking questions . . . seeking answers . . . awed by the mystery of life . . . carrying the flare of our divinity into the darkness. As it turns out, we discover that our hunger to experience the Presence is really the Presence's own hunger to experience Itself!

3

A Global Community

The great religions of the world are searching their histories and examining their positions. Bit by bit, pieces of the past are falling away and things are moving more toward commonality than difference. A global synthesis is coalescing, and it feels "right." Heading home . . . moving toward oneness—it's the way of the world. We are witnessing the coming together of a worldwide community.

The global community being established is not a political one or an economic one, a racial one or a religious one. It is a *spiritual* one. It is a worldwide community of pray-ers—people who pray—because prayer is one thing common to people everywhere.

Loren Eiseley continues:

> The need is not really for more
> brains, the need is now for a gentler,
> a more tolerant people than those
> who won for us against the ice, the
> tiger, and the bear. The hand that
> hefted the ax, out of some old blind
> allegiance to the past fondles the
> machine gun as lovingly. It is a habit
> [we] will have to break to survive,
> but the roots go very deep.[3]

The Homecoming

The book in your hand is part of a series that probes more deeply into the uncharted territory of our inner world. The journey we are on—our quest for spiritual rediscovery—leads us finally back to ourselves. Like the prodigal son, we have spent enough time in the far country and long to come home—to that sanctuary of peace within our souls where, in timeless stillness, we come face-to-face with the Truth that we and God are one. Craving this "homecoming"—this return to the promised land— we search for the trail which will lead us there.

Prayer is that trail.

Directions

Our lives lose direction the moment they cease to be a voyage for the discovery of God.
—Author Unknown[4]

Quest for Prayer can be utilized on many levels. It is up to you to decide how far and how deeply you wish to go with it. Each chapter begins with a discussion of a topic and then moves into an Adventure segment which will serve as a bridge to help you transport the philosophical aspect into your everyday life. As in the original books of the series, *The Quest* and *Adventures on the Quest,* each of these two segments is designed to supplement and complement the other.

Read and study the discussion segment first, doing your best to understand the concept(s) presented. If you are part of a study group, be sure to bring up for discussion any questions you may have and any points you think are important.

Next, read the Adventure segment and answer all the questions and do all the activities. If given a written assignment, it's really important to do the actual writing because writing helps you focus your thoughts and more accurately identify your feelings. (Merely thinking about an answer or only verbalizing it is not really enough.)

Also, intellectually understanding a concept is not enough either. Incorporating it into your life is what really counts, and the only way to accomplish this is with continual practice.

You will notice that each Adventure segment has certain activities in common. These require you to take specific actions and are designed to clarify further and/or to integrate into your life more fully the concept being discussed. Each Adventure will present the following:

Soul-Talk

This is a call to action! Each is a short affirmative statement designed to increase your awareness of the concept under discussion. Make each one a verbal companion the entire time you are working on the chapter. Silently or aloud, repeat your *Soul-Talk* statement as many times as you think of it during the day. But to begin with, write it out three times. Do this S-L-O-W-L-Y, taking ten or fifteen seconds between each writing so that you can better assimilate the meaning of the statement and the impact it may have on your life.

Soul-Thoughts

After writing your *Soul-Talk*, become quiet and give free reign to any thoughts and feelings that come to mind. Gently note any impressions you get about the current *Soul-Thought* or current concept and write them down.

The more open you are to your spontaneous thoughts and the more honestly you write them down in this section, the richer your experience will be. This then will become a living journal of your personal quest to make prayer a more important part of your life.

Off the Main Trail

For those desiring to go deeper, here is an optional activity designed to "stretch" the soul. This is not part of the regular Adventure, and you have the choice of following where it leads or moving directly to the next chapter.

Stepping-Stone

Each Adventure segment ends with a small task to perform. These are simple changes in lifestyle designed to pave the way for larger, more meaningful changes. Just as adding a touch of color to a can of paint will change the color of the entire can, so little changes in our lives lead the way to changing our entire lives.

To summarize:

1. **Read** both the discussion segment and the Adventure segment.
2. **Soul-Talk:** Write the *Soul-Talk* three times, pausing between each time. Use the phrase as often as you think of it while working with the chapter.
3. **Soul-Thoughts:** After writing your *Soul-Thoughts,* write out your thoughts and feelings.
4. **Activities:** Do them all! Be as open and as honest and as thorough as possible.
5. **Off the Main Trail:** Journey if you are feeling extra adventuresome.

6. **Stepping-Stone:** Use the *Stepping-Stone* each day for the entire time you are covering the chapter.

For a base camp from which to venture forth on your Quest for Prayer, we refer you to the original work—the foundation of the Continuing Quest series—*The Quest* and *Adventures on the Quest*.

Chapter One

When we pray, it is the
Mind of God seeking to
fullfill Itself as us.

The What and Why
of Prayer

"As a deer longs for flowing streams,
so my soul longs for you, O God."
—Psalm 42:1

There is something comforting about taking
time out to commune with a Higher Power. There
is something indescribably exquisite in savoring
the sweet luxury of special moments of conscious
awareness of God. The soul naturally seeks the experience of raising itself to a spiritual level, where
it can think and feel from its inner core of divinity.
It is these heightened moments which satisfy—
which give us the strength to go forward, the joy to
warm our hearts, the comfort to ease our sorrows.
When human circumstances seem to overwhelm,
when we grow frustrated with our lives, confused
as to our choices, or mystified at our place in this
vast universe, we ultimately turn to prayer.

Basically, we pray simply because we cannot do otherwise! Nothing else works. "All things pray, and all things pour forth their souls. The heavens pray, the earth prays, every creature and every living thing. In all life, there is longing. Creation is itself but a longing, a kind of prayer to the Almighty. What are the clouds, the rising and the setting of the sun, the soft radiance of the moon and the gentleness of the night? What are the flashes of the human mind and the storms of the human heart? They are all prayers—the outpouring of boundless longing for God."[5]

A Deliberate Activity

Prayer is a deliberate activity—one of seeking to recognize our oneness with God, of opening ourselves to the power of God as it moves through us in new and wonderful ways. Prayer is a yearning as old as creation—a desire to feel reconnected with that which made us and sustains us all. Prayer is born of a longing, a need. We are empty and long to be filled. We seek solace in things and relationships until they all fail us. Eventually, we know only God can fill us. We have no choice but to pray because our other choices, the choices born of our well-intentioned but puny intellectual efforts to know God, are hopelessly inadequate. Prayer, then, in its simplest form is any conscious attempt to experience the presence of God.

But this is only the beginning. As we seek through prayer to know God, our awareness of God *as* us increases and expands. And as prayer fills us more and more, we become more and more aware of the experience of being part of God. This means that as we pray, we are drawn inexorably into the creative flow of the universe, so that we begin perceiving things not with human eyes or human ears or human minds but from the absolute core of us—the divinity within us. As we approach this point in our prayer life, the emphasis of our prayers begins to make a subtle shift. Rather than praying *to* God to help us or *for* God to be with us, we begin praying *from* that sacred presence which is our very essence. So we can say, then, that when we pray, we are lifting our personal identity to a higher awareness—the awareness that *it is God that is praying!* When we pray, it is the mind of God seeking to fulfill itself as us.

So the longing that we feel to "come home" to Spirit is Spirit Itself calling us to awaken, to open our hearts and see what is in there, and once having seen, to let It come forth into our everyday world.

Most People Pray

Since the beginning of time, people of all civilizations have prayed. From pious silence to emotional shouts of "Amen," from fondled prayer beads

to spinning prayer wheels, from solemn and measured Gregorian chanting to foot-stomping, hand-
clapping gospel music, from a crowd of fervent
worshipers flogging their backs with ropes to the
solitary seeker quietly sitting cross-legged atop a
mountain—there are as many ways of praying as
there are people who pray.

According to Eric Butterworth, the word *prayer*
has its roots in the ancient Sanskrit word *pal-al*,
which means "judging oneself to be wondrously
made."[6] While a surprising 90 percent of the people in the United States pray, according to a Gallup
poll, and 60 percent of these people consider
prayer to be very important to their daily lives,[7] it's
doubtful that a majority of them consider themselves to be "wondrously made." And yet they are!
We all are! In fact, at the root of our reason for
praying is the need for us to know just how wondrously we are made.

Verbal and Meditative Prayer

While each prayer can be different, there are basically two ways of praying—verbally and meditatively. Verbal prayers involve words, spoken or unspoken. These words take the form of thanksgiving
("Thank You, God, for my new car and my wonderful family and my new job . . ."), petition
("Praise be to Allah, Creator of the worlds. Thee do

we worship, and Thee do we ask for aid."), inter-
cession ("Dear Blessed Mother, in your heavenly
mercy, ask your Son, Jesus, to help me."), praise
("God, You are so great and good. I love You."), rit-
ual (e.g. chanting the same words over and over),
and conversation directly with God (speaking with
God as you would a friend).

Meditative prayer, on the other hand, is more
personal, more inner-directed. In fact, it is the ultimate personal and personalized communication
with God. Like a distinct and private megahertz
frequency on a radio band, it is uniquely our own.

Often referred to as the prayer of the heart, meditation involves waiting in silence with usually no
other purpose than to experience oneness with
God. According to a Gallup poll, people who use
meditative prayer seem to have a more intense experience of God than those who use verbal prayer.[8]
This should not be surprising since meditative
prayer is by its very nature the quintessence of personal prayer.

However, *any* means of prayer which opens our
hearts to that mystical experience of the Creator
expressing Itself as us is valid, very individual, and
highly personal. Spending time in stillness, in silence, with the sole purpose of becoming more
aware of God in our lives is a most powerful experience. When we consider the sense of expectation

and excitement one would have in meeting a
world-famous figure or a powerful king or world
ruler, we can get a tiny hint of the sense of exhila-
ration of the time spent in meditation, of seeking to
increase an awareness of the Creator of this universe. It is powerful indeed.

Verbal or meditative, in any language, any pos-
ture, any form—prayer is part of life. *God is seeking us.* Having given us the gift of free will, however, God does not command us to seek God first.
This Power simply awaits our recognition of It.
Anytime we do anything that is consciously directed toward opening the door to the experience
of oneness, we are praying. When that door can remain permanently open, our entire lives become a
prayer.

Mile Markers

- Prayer, in its simplest form, is any conscious attempt to experience the presence of God.

- As we seek through prayer to know God, our awareness of God *as* us increases and expands.

- It is God that is praying.

- There are as many ways of praying as there are people who pray.

- Two basic ways of praying are verbally and meditatively.

- *Any* means of prayer which opens our hearts to that mystical experience of the Creator expressing Itself as us is valid.

- God is seeking us.

Beloved Creator, my only prayer is to know Your presence in my life. You are my breath, my thoughts, my very existence—now and always.

Adventure One

The What and Why
of Prayer

Certain thoughts are prayers. There are
moments when, whatever be the attitude
of the body, the soul is on its knees.

—Victor Hugo[9]

Sheik Nasruddin was crossing the desert on his
camel. By nightfall it was very chilly so he stopped,
erected his tent, and tried to fall asleep. Shivering
in the cold, he was astonished to hear his camel
outside; "Master, I am very cold. May I please sleep
in your tent tonight?"

"Preposterous!" said Nasruddin. "There's hardly
enough room for me. Where would I put you?"

He closed his eyes, still shaking in the cool night
air, but was again interrupted by the camel.

"Master," said the camel, "perhaps I could just
put my nose under the flap of the tent. That may
keep me from freezing to death."

"Okay," grumbled Nasruddin. "You can put your
nose in here if it makes you feel better."

And so the camel edged the flap up and wedged his soft nose into the tent. Nasruddin tried to sleep again only to be interrupted again by the camel.

"I am so sorry to disturb you, Master, but now that my nose is warm my ears feel colder. Could I just edge in a bit more so that my ears will be warm?"

Nasruddin was so desperate for sleep that, just to quiet the camel, he agreed. "What's a few more inches?" he said to himself. But when the camel's ears were in the tent the camel wanted his neck warmer. This was done, and as more requests were made and agreed upon, more and more of the camel entered the tent.

This continued for about an hour as, little by little, the camel insinuated himself into the tent. Finally, although there was little room left over, both Nasruddin and the camel were in the tent, warm and cuddly. Nasruddin, using the camel's neck as a pillow, had the best sleep of his life.

We pray . . . God blesses us. Many think this is all that prayer is about, that this is how prayer should work. Yet God's blessings are already abundantly available in our lives, and the greatest blessing we are given is the will to know God, the desire to experience the divine reality of what we are and what our relationship to God is. And once the flame of that desire takes hold in us, once the "camel's nose is under the tent," it really doesn't matter why we pray, how we pray, when we pray, where we pray, or for what we pray. We can beseech God or chant to God or meditate in the silence or talk to God as we would talk to a friend. We can pray on our knees or our stomachs, we can pray standing, sitting, on our backs, or on our heads. Nor does it matter what we say. All that really matters is *that* we pray.

Spending conscious time striving to expand our experience of God is what matters. Living our everyday lives seeking more and more of an awareness of God in all that we do is the crucial component. The more we can become aware of God as us, the more we will align our lives to be in tune with this great Presence and Its will for us. Then, in the flow of the Infinite, our lives are harmonized and we come to realize we live immersed in a veritable sea of blessings.

The more we pray, the easier praying becomes. Each time we say or think a prayer, each day we live our lives with an awareness of God, more of the camel is sliding under the tent until finally we are "sleeping with the camel"—finally, all of our world is taken up with prayer.

Soul-Talk

I live a life of prayer.

1. _____

2. _____

3. _____

Soul-Thoughts

Living a life of prayer is possible, but it's not nec-
essarily easy. In fact, living a life of prayer may be
the most difficult quest we can attempt. When we
think of living a life of prayer, we may think of
monks or nuns living lives of quiet contemplation.

Yet one's life, no matter where it is lived, can be a prayer if one is aware of the presence of God. So if each time we think of it, we become aware of God's presence in our lives, then we are living a life of prayer.

1. Discuss how it is possible for people to live a life of prayer and still exist in the world of business and commerce. For example, *how can a lawyer or accountant or construction worker or secretary do this?*

2. Discuss the specifics of what adjustments you can make in your life and in your job to live a life of prayer.

3. Discuss to what extent your relationships—family, social, and business—can help or hinder your living a life of prayer.

4. Comment on this statement: "We pray because we cannot do otherwise."

Off the Main Trail

Take an extensive inventory of the important things in your life—family, friends, job, possessions, habits, likes, and dislikes—and note whether they help or hinder your living a life of prayer. Be specific *in making a plan to change in some way all the things that don't help you.*

Stepping-Stone

   Make a *conscious* effort every day this week to be aware of how you are acting. Before going to bed at night, replay your day, noting whether you reacted to every encounter in a God-centered, kind, loving, and compassionate way. Critique *(do not criticize)* yourself so you can be more effective next time a similar situation presents itself.

I live a life of prayer.

Chapter Two

There is only one sure way
of proving to ourselves that
our prayers are effective.

How to Pray

> "We do not know how to pray as we ought,
> but that very Spirit intercedes with sighs
> too deep for words."
>
> —Romans 8:26

Virtually every religion embraces some form of prayer, and followers of each religion are told to pray. But seldom are they taught *how* to pray, and so most people are troubled by doubts about whether they have been praying correctly.

A great many people view prayer as a way to get things—a healing, a new relationship, a certain house, a job, and so forth—and they want to know how to pray effectively so they can see specific results from their efforts.

But "getting things" is not the ultimate purpose of prayer. The true purpose of prayer is to experience God. The highest use of prayer, then, is to announce our intention of opening ourselves to the presence of God. It is our endeavor to merge with and accept all the qualities of God—a heartfelt invitation to allow God's life to be lived through us.

Therefore, in order to pray "effectively," we don't have to pray specifically to change people or circumstances. We pray to experience God. Yet the interesting result of our praying to experience God is that the people and circumstances in our lives *do* change! Why? Because prayer has changed *us*. Secure in an awareness of God's presence, we then deal with the people and the circumstances of our lives in more loving ways. Prayer—seeking more awareness of God living as us—changes *us*, and in changing us changes all aspects of our lives.

What great news, because it means there is no need to beg God for anything, since we already have access to all that God is! Of course, if we're in a situation where all we feel we can do is beg, there is nothing wrong with that. Yet prayer can be so much more. When prayer becomes the way to express our thanks for life and its blessings—those we are already aware of and those still to be discovered— it is sometimes referred to as "affirmative prayer." Such prayer acknowledges the Truth that God is present in us and in every situation, and therefore the potential for us is beyond anything we can humanly imagine.

Let's look at an example. If we are praying

specifically for more prosperity, for instance, we may attain it simply because we are focusing our energy on prosperity and making it a priority in our lives. Undoubtedly, strongly focused mental will can often produce the results we're looking for. But that only opens us to one portion of what there is for us to experience. It's like ordering only a beverage from a menu full of wonderful food. We have limited ourselves and may not be fully open to all the rest—health, love, joy, peace, and the teeming font of absolute soul satisfaction, which is available simply because we are part of the presence of God.

The Real Search

Can "things" ever really satisfy our souls? Sooner or later we realize that true satisfaction comes only from finding God. As Charles Fillmore, cofounder of Unity, declared: "The real search of all people is for God. They may think they are looking for other things, but they must eventually admit that it is God they seek."[10]

While historically we may have prayed to a Higher Power outside ourselves, imploring for things and outer changes in our lives, we are now discovering that this Power we thought was someplace "out there," is omnipresent and lives as each of us.

As a separated drop of ocean water eventually makes its way back to the sea, we are inexorably drawn back into the awareness of our oneness with God. The drop of water may evaporate from the ocean and be drawn into the clouds to be blown by the wind and fall as snow on the highest mountain. Eventually the snow will melt and the drop will become part of a trickle and then a stream and then a river until finally it returns to the sea. If we could suspend reason for a moment, we might imagine that at various points in its journey the drop may pray to melt or to be part of the trickle, or it may pray to join a stream or a river. But what it *really* "wants" is to find the ocean again.

Our prayers are to find God again—to be lifted by Spirit as It speaks and thinks and acts *as us*.

There is a Hasidic tale which describes a poor farmer making his way back from the market when a wheel of his cart falls off. Stranded in the woods, he is distressed because he is without his prayer book and will not be able to say his prayers that day.

Desiring so strongly to pray, he decides to improvise: "I have been foolish, God, for I left home this morning without my prayer book, and my memory is so poor I cannot pray without the book. So I shall recite the alphabet five times very slowly and You, who knows all prayers, can arrange the letters to form the prayers I cannot remember."

And God says, "Of all the prayers I have heard

today, this one was the best because it came from a
simple and sincere heart." [11]

One cannot help being reminded of Jesus' directions for how to pray: "When you are praying, do
not heap up empty phrases . . . . For your Father
knows what you need before you ask him." [12]

The "Right" Method?

What exactly is the *right* method of prayer? There
are as many *right* methods of praying as there are
people who pray! More important than the method
of praying is the *reason* for praying. Prayers are not
to change God, as we know. They are to change us—
to lift us into the experience of the presence of God.

The Creator cares about, sustains, maintains, and
expresses Itself through the created. God is waiting
for us to open ourselves to the sacred Presence being
lived through us. God is waiting for us to express
our willingness to be guided and nurtured. Therefore, one of our prayers might be to express this willingness: *"Here I am, God. Live Your life through me."*

By opening our hearts to the love already there,
by expressing our willingness to let the sacred
Presence live through us, we take a big step in getting into a prayer mode. We each will do this in our
own ways, of course, but a helpful means of prepar-
ing for our prayer experience is to relax the body,

breathe easily, and turn the attention inward. And while there is no one "secret" method of prayer, the acknowledgment of the presence of God is always a meaningful way to begin. This may take the form of words, aloud or silent.

What kind of words? Remember that we are talking to a friend, really our best friend, so we should speak whatever is in our hearts. Praying is a very simple activity and requires no special words—only the willingness, the hunger, to know God. Whatever phrases, in any language, spoken or unspoken, that help move us into the place deep within our souls where we can begin to feel our oneness with God— these are prayers. (Some sample prayers are included later in the book.)

Beyond Words

Eventually, however, we move beyond words— beyond thoughts—into the vaster realm of pure Spirit. This is what is sometimes called "the silence." During our times of prayer, we discover what is waiting in that utter silence to be discovered. We dip into the eternal wellspring of divine life that exists within us. And there, in the absolute stillness, we simply rest in the exquisite sense of the presence of God.

During our quiet times of prayer we may want to let go of any preconceived ideas, any doubts, any desired outcomes, and surrender ourselves completely to God. If we find a parade of thoughts marching by as we sit in stillness, we can merely become indifferent to them, just allowing them to pass through and then gently bringing our focus back to the inner silence. Nonresistance is the key here so that we remain tranquil and able to savor the experience. (Sometimes this is easier said than done. Often our thoughts are like mischievous monkeys darting in and out of our conscious awareness. However, as long as we don't resist them but gently keep directing our focus back to center, our minds will eventually become more and more quiet.)

"The secret place of the Most High" is an inner space, a very personal place of total silence, which no one else can ever enter or disturb. It is this eternal, changeless part of us that waits like a safe harbor to welcome us in calm or storm, in peace or turmoil. It is in the silence that we feel infused with God. It is in the silence that we find our peace and our strength, our joy and our healing.

A few moments in utter stillness quickly bring us back to the realization that we are part of our Creator, part of the universe, and that truly we are not alone.

Phases of Prayer

While everyone will pray and experience God in unique ways and while there is no one way to pray, there are some very broad guidelines that can be helpful to those of us whose main purpose in praying is to experience God. This process can be distilled into three basic phases.

1. **Surrender.** We begin with a willingness to surrender all of our wishes, hopes, and expectations. We become willing to just . . . let . . . go. Why? Because as long as we are holding on, we are directing. Letting go is letting God direct. Something beyond our greatest dreams will happen when we surrender completely to God. All the superficial goings-on of our human lives are put aside when we actually pray from a consciousness of God. When we surrender to God, we are allowing God's will to prevail.

But surrender, although simple in concept, is rarely easy to do. Frankly, true surrender is often *extremely* difficult. At first we may find we're not able to surrender totally or even a little bit. But what we can do totally and completely is be *willing* to surrender. Our willingness to surrender, our desire to let go, opens the door for God to direct our lives.

2. **Be Still.** The second phase of prayer is simply waiting, waiting in that perfect stillness, in silence, and allowing Spirit to fully possess us. In this phase, we actually become more consciously aware of the presence of God. This is a time of few or no words, where the strength and peace of God can permeate our lives.This is a time of sitting completely still, de-

siring to be aware of nothing except the presence of God. It cannot be forced. Our only responsibility is to quietly make ourselves available.

Just as fully surrendering is difficult, so initially can be sitting in perfect stillness. Thoughts are constantly floating by, various parts of our body seek attention, outside noises intervene, even our breathing or heartbeat can distract us. Again, it is not the perfect stillness that is critical, it is our *willingness* to become still, to listen only to the still small voice, and to make ourselves available. With our willingness and perseverence come the beginnings of stillness and silence. This phase, when achieved, is outside of the dimensions of time and space as we know them. We simply are.

3. **Let God.** Once we sense our time in the stillness is over, whether that was two minutes or thirty, the process of prayer has not ended. We now are in the glow of prayer—a higher state of consciousness, of awareness. In this glow, we can now bring what we experienced into our everyday activities. Lifted by knowing that God is our very life and that *God is seeking us*, we now remain entirely open to God by holding onto the transcendent perspective we gained in the silence. In this third phase, we allow ourselves to be acted upon by Spirit in our everyday lives in whatever way Spirit wishes to express Itself through us. We let go and let God.

We no longer ask for things, but instead become conduits through which divine energy can more freely be released. We synchronize ourselves with the cosmic flow, which is another way of describing God's willingness to express through us. Let us make no mistake—the potential for healing, or whatever else, is always there. But now our role is simply to acknowledge it and rest in that awareness, and then to get on with life and operate in the complete trust that the process is working.

When we speak now, it is God speaking as us. This is the *real* "spoken word." Our words are not generated by superficial desires and pleading, which often take the form of repetitive statements powered only by the force of our own human will. What is our human will, when compared to God's will? Now our "spoken word" will rise up out of the very presence of Spirit in our hearts and will move to establish the divine plan throughout creation and in our own lives.

A Further Word About the "Spoken Word"

The "Spoken Word" has nothing to do with trying to manipulate people and circumstances or make things happen. Words themselves are essentially arrangements of letters of the alphabet and have no power of their own. When attached to strong ideas and feelings, however, and when spoken from our highest consciousness of God, they possess power— the power of the Infinite. These *true* spoken words are devoid of any ego or personal will and are actually a release of the power of God within us! Such words have the power to change us and therefore our circumstances.

Always at Home

The whole idea of the prayer process is to help us realize what the Prodigal Son finally realized—that no matter what we have done or how far we think we may have strayed, the Father is always at home . . . waiting. Waiting for us to return. And not only eternally waiting, but eternally longing to live freely through us.

And so we come to see that the purpose of prayer is not to fill an earthly need—new job, better relationship, healing—but to satisfy the natural longing in our souls, not only to experience our Creator but actually to live from that experience. Even if we do pray for specific things, the underlying need is really the need to *experience* our spirituality, to *feel* our oneness with God, to *sense* the comfort and the guidance and the healing that rise up out of opening ourselves to God. For it is not we who are doing the praying or the seeking, it is God!

Proof of Success

There is only one sure way of proving to ourselves that our prayers are effective. Are we acting with loving kindness toward each other and all creation? This is the true sign of effective prayer, if we want to think of prayer in terms of success or failure.

It would seem that if we have gone through the three phases—surrendering, becoming still, and then letting God express fully in our daily activities—we will be experiencing joy, peace, trust, compassion, and feelings of connection with all humankind. It would seem that these are the marks of people who let God be God in their lives.

> There is a light that shines beyond
>   all things on earth, beyond us all,
>   beyond the heavens, beyond the
>   highest, the very highest heavens.
>   This is the light that shines in our
>   hearts.
>   —Chandogya Upanishad[13]

Always Available

There are numerous opportunities every day to still the body and quiet the mind, allowing us to slip between the cracks of our outer world and into the inner one of silence. It might be in the quiet of the early morning or during some wordless moments of a prayer service or even during those brief (but seemingly eternal!) moments when we sit in noisy traffic waiting for the light to turn green! The stillness, in other words, is always available.

If we are newcomers to prayer and communion with God and are harassed by thoughts, feelings, and memories during times of prayer, it is important not to give up. By making it a daily habit to become consciously aware of the presence of God, it becomes easier and easier. Each prayer experience builds upon the previous one, having a cumulative effect. Ultimately, through prayer, we will be transformed into the God-centered beings we are meant to be. Our "joy will be full," for we will be experiencing the unimaginable wonder of God, as it expresses itself through our lives.

Mile Markers

- The true purpose of prayer is to experience God.

- More important than the method of praying is the *reason* for praying.

- God is waiting for our willingness to be guided and nurtured.

- During our times of prayer, we discover what is waiting in the utter silence to be discovered.

- During our quiet times of prayer, we let go any preconceived ideas, and surrender completely to God.

- Three basic phases of prayer are surrender, stillness, and letting God.

- The *real* "Spoken Word" is God speaking to us.

- Our acting with loving kindness is the one sure proof that our prayers are effective.

Sacred Spirit of Life, I surrender myself completely to Your divine plan. As I sit in stillness, I sense Your powerful presence moving in me and my world. Thank You for guiding me every step of my way.

Adventure Two

How to Pray

Just to be is a blessing.
Just to live is holy.
—Rabbi Abraham Heschel[14]

Years ago, when the circus came to town, the clowns, acrobats, musicians, and other entertainers along with many of the animals would parade down Main Street in order to drum up enthusiasm. The elephants were always among the favorites, and many people would try to feed them peanuts as they lumbered by. But since stopping to eat would slow down the parade, the animal trainers taught each elephant to hold on to the tail of the elephant in front of it with its trunk. With their trunks thus engaged, the elephants could not stop to feed.

Like an elephant's trunk, our minds often need to be otherwise engaged when we are seeking the silence. Thoughts flicker in and out, intruding on our attempt at stillness and silence. Often concentrating on our breathing or reciting a specific phrase over and over will serve as a means of keeping the mind centered.

We concentrate on our breathing by becoming aware of each inhalation and exhalation. We let our minds follow the breath, focusing on its rhythm and allowing it to flow in and out naturally, as it wishes. In other words, we do not alter our breathing, we simply observe it. This serves to keep the mind away from distractions and therefore more open to the presence of Spirit. Some people find it helpful to begin their quiet time by thinking of each inhalation as the breath of Spirit filling the lungs with new life and the exhalation as the release of stale air, disease, negative emotions, or anything else no longer needed by the person.

Others who find using a specific phrase or word or sound as a way of staying centered might say or whisper, for example, *Holy* as they inhale and *Spirit* as they exhale. Whatever words or sounds are chosen, there are three points worth noting:

1. The same words or sounds should be used each time so they become a signal to the mind that this is a special prayer time.
2. Words or sounds can be uttered aloud, whispered, or spoken internally.
3. Words or sounds should be synchronized with the natural rhythm of the breath. Whatever our words

or sounds, if they succeed in bringing us to a point where we communicate with God in silence, then they are effective prayers.

But let's be realistic. We all know there are times when our lives are so confused, so hurtful, so up-side-down, that lamentations and complaints to God are about all we are capable of uttering. What to do? God's promise to you is that your very desire to be lifted out of this dark period is enough to get you eventually back on track. Trust that promise. Hang on to it as you would a floating raft in a shipwreck, for eventually it will bring you safely to shore.

Soul-Talk

Here I am, God. Live your life through me.

1. _____

2. _____

3. _____

Soul-Thoughts

Praying for "things" may eventually allow some to know God. But it is a long and circuitous route. Usually by praying for "things," we only know things. To know God, there must be a conscious desire to know God and then a conscious surrender to the presence of God. That is what prayer is.

1. *How were you taught to pray? How does it differ from how you pray now?*

2. Has anything you prayed hard for led you to know more of God in your life?

3. Have you ever been angry that God did not "answer your prayer" or happy that God did "answer your prayer"? Explain.

Did you love God more or less in either of these instances?

*Did you feel God loved you more or less
in either of these instances?*

What of Miracles?

Sometimes we get results from prayer that are far
beyond what we would have expected. We call them
miracles. But "miracles" are what happen when we
get ourselves out of the way so that the activity of
God can work freely. It is like removing the dam in
a brook so that the water can tumble and flow where
it will. What we call "miracles" are really natural
outworkings of the activity of God, even when they
take place instantaneously.

The danger in focusing on the traditional concept
of miracles is that if we believe we need a miracle
in order to have something change in our lives (or
someone else's), if we feel that only a miracle can
help, then we are automatically limiting the power
of our prayers. In focusing too specifically, we are
ignoring the fact that the very nature of God is
wholeness, abundance, and love. As part of God's
creation, we already have access to all that. To tap
into these attributes is natural, not miraculous. To
pray for a miracle is to see a cosmic lottery where
wholeness, abundance, and love are the exceptions
and not the rule.

4. *Why do you think people need to believe in miracles?*

5. *What does a belief in miracles indicate about one's belief in God?*

God's Laws

Prayer does not make us immune to the divine laws of nature and the universe. God has fashioned all creations according to laws. Let's not make the mistake of assuming that because we are expressions of God—part of the presence of God—we are immune to God's laws. God's laws apply to *all* creation. Praying the "Prayer for Protection" before stepping off a cliff does not exempt us from the law of gravity, saying grace before eating unhealthful food does not exempt us from the laws of nutrition, sitting in silence and experiencing oneness with God before angrily mistreating another person does not exempt us from the basic commandment of love.

6. *Do you feel it is reasonable to flaunt the rules of health and ask God for healing?*

7. *In reference to question 6, what is the most inconsistent behavior you have linked with your prayers?*

Off the Main Trail

 Refer back to the section in this chapter entitled "Proof of Success." Keep a log indicating how your own daily behavior offers proof of the "success" or "failure" of your prayers.

Stepping-Stone

 Every day this week, consciously send loving thoughts to the first stranger you run across. You don't have to speak. Just consciously love the person.

God's life is being lived through me.

Chapter Three

Prayer is a way for God
to get *our* attention.

Praying for Ourselves

> Let my soul ever seek you, and let me persist
> in seeking, till I have found and am in full
> possession of you.
>
> —Saint Augustine[15]

There are as many ways of praying as there are people who pray, and there are as many *reasons* for praying as there are people who pray: new jobs, healing, prosperity, better relationships, letting go of harmful habits, selling homes, better bosses, winning the lottery—people even pray for harm to come to an "enemy." Imagine how busy God would be, sorting and cataloging those billions of individual prayer requests received each day! And then there is that matter of priority and worthiness to be established and the particular changes of circumstances needed to grant the prayer request. What would God do, for example, when the pious farmer prays for rain but the organizers of the annual church picnic in the same town pray for sunny skies? What of a basketball game where both sides pray to win?

We all have needs and probably, from time to time, have prayed about those needs. But if we're playing "Let's Make a Deal" with God, like, "God, I promise to go to church every Sunday if I win the lottery," then prayer is not a spiritual activity but a negotiation, a business deal. Where is the awareness of God in our lives in such a contractual prayer?

In *The Quest* and *Adventures on the Quest,* we spoke of this and other kinds of manipulative prayers— prayers of supplication where we believe that groveling low enough and long enough will make God have pity on us and grant our requests, prayers of flattery in which we assume a vain God would hear us, or repetitive prayers said in the hope of getting an otherwise unattentive God's attention. We concluded that these were not prayers so much as attempts to get what we want by trying to manipulate God.

A Better Question

Before asking how to pray for ourselves, perhaps a better question would be, "Do we really *need* to pray for ourselves?" One of the dilemmas inherent in praying for specific things is that our attention is directed away from God and focused on the problem. Our lives become centered on that certain set of worrisome circumstances—the house that won't sell, the wife that is drinking excessively, layoffs at work, the apprehension about the result of medical tests. Each prayer time, rather than being a time when we simply surrender to the Power living Its life as us, becomes a time of apprehension and concern. Praying for such specific outcomes keeps us caught up in the problem—keeps us on the level of the problem—and so our prayers actually become a more profound form of worry.

Secondly, praying for things assumes we can manipulate God with our words and logic. This implies that God is some subservient and separate being amenable to a *quid pro quo*! It also implies that God was responsible for the problem in the first place and thus should take it away.

And lastly, praying to God to change a specific circumstance takes us away from any sense of oneness with God. Rather than praying from a conscious unity *with* God, we are praying from a sense of separation *from* God. Praying for things assumes that God is separate from us, has something we want, and may give it to us (depending on what we say and how we act!). The truth of the matter is that what we are really seeking is not anything more than a fuller awareness of the God-life being lived as us. Our very asking God for something indicates that in our own minds we have separated God from ourselves.

To Pray or Not to Pray?

So we are faced with two questions. One—if our problems should not be included in our prayers, what do we do about our problems? And two—*should* we even pray for ourselves?

If we remember that praying is not about God or about what God can do for us, then the answer to both these questions becomes clear. Praying is about our consciousness or our awareness of God. Praying for things has nothing to do with God; it has to do with trying to manipulate circumstances to gratify our sense of order—*our* perception of how things should be in our world. When they are not to our liking, we pray to God to "make it right, make it my way."

However, when we can open ourselves to God's greater plan for us—and *trust* that plan even when circumstances may appear to the contrary—then we are allowing God to live freely as us, and that divine plan will unfold itself.

Pitfalls of Prayer

Time for a *caveat* here—time to address the potential pitfalls of prayer. Yes, God desires to live freely as us. And yes, the divine plan will unfold itself if we open ourselves to it. But just as a mighty river can bring new life to the parched land and at the same time stir up old silt and debris needing to be washed away, a fervently embarked-upon life of prayer waters the soul but may also stir up old "stuff."

Emilie Cady termed this phenomenon *chemicalization* in her book *Lessons in Truth.*[16] The soul collects a vast number of attitudes, beliefs, and experiences over the course of its immortal journey. Usually this collection contains things that need to be brought to the light and flushed out. Prayer has the ability to do this, and sometimes the process creates a seeming upheaval in our lives while the cleansing is taking place. A symptom or condition may be temporarily exacerbated, for instance. And so we anguish over why, when we are finally living a spiritual life, do things suddenly seem to get worse?

Temporary is the key word here, and that's why, should anyone ever encounter this kind of experience, it is crucial to "hang in there" and persist with prayer and great trust. Right in the very face of the upheaval, we must stand absolutely firm in our belief that God is at work. Eventually, things smooth out and life is better than it *ever* was! In fact, there's a chance it might not bear close resemblance to the former life at all. If so, *it will be wonderful.* We can count on that.

Not everyone experiences such turmoil when starting down the prayer path—most people do not. But we mention it "just in case."

We Are the Avenues

How do we pray for ourselves? In answering that, let's first remember that prayer is not a way for us to get God's attention! On the contrary, prayer is a way for God to get *our* attention. And once we surrender to the Sacred Presence, there *is only* the Presence—nothing to do, nothing to ask. God is enough because God is all. Out of this realization come more blessings than we could ever wish for. All God's blessings are ours *right now*! We don't have to ask for them in prayer.

And lastly, let's remember that God is a creative process that is forever in search of avenues of expression. We are those avenues. To spend our prayer time asking God for something we think we need is to deny the full magnificent scope of God in our lives. Doesn't it make more sense to trust that this Power which created the entire universe knows what is best? After all, we would not be so arrogant as to think *we* can see a bigger picture than God!

Mile Markers

- Our very asking for something indicates that in our own minds we have separated God from ourselves.
- Praying for things has nothing to do with God.
- Prayer is a way for God to get *our* attention.
- All God's blessings are ours *right now.*
- God is a creative process that is forever in search of avenues of expression. We are those avenues.

Thank You, God, for the richness of life. You are all I need . . . You are all I want. May each moment of my life be a prayer of thanksgiving for Your sacred presence.

Adventure Three

Praying for Ourselves

One of the best ways to worship
God is simply to be happy.
—Traditional Hindu wisdom[17]

If we feel we alone know best what is good and
bad for us and if we pray for these things and in-
vest our emotions in the outcome of our prayers,
then our happiness will always be dependent on outcomes. Circumstances that we cannot control and
will never be able to control will always be in charge.

However, if we feel deep in our hearts that we are
a part of God and God is part of us, then what happens to us doesn't dictate our lives. In fact, if we
live from an awareness of being centered in God,
things can't happen *to* us, they can only happen *as*
us!

Soul-Talk

God lives as me.

1. _____

2. _____

3. _____

Soul-Thoughts

Things Just "Are!"

Things don't go "right" or "wrong" in our lives. Things just are. Circumstances and events are neutral and have no power in themselves. However, our reaction to a circumstance or event may be "right"

or "wrong." In using our judgment, we decide when
and if an event or circumstance affecting our life is
a negative or positive one. Then we tailor our prayers
to reflect our judgment. But how can we know for
sure? Given the vast number of variables in our lives
now and the infinite and unknowable variables in
our future, the tiny window of our intellect and
senses that we look through in each now moment
is too narrow to give us anything but the most mea-
ger hint of our needs. What we *can* know is that God
knows best. Trusting God, turning over our care,
concern, fear, and worry to God, then, becomes not
only the most intelligent thing we can do, it is really our only choice.

> 1. There are circumstances in our lives
> that we feel are important and perhaps
> even critical to our happiness. Maybe it's
> a need for healing or enough money to
> pay the rent or a better relationship with
> someone. Identify one circumstance in
> your life right now that prompts you to
> pray to God for help.

2. Rather than praying for a specific outcome in the challenge you are presently facing, write a prayer that will center you in the flow of God's perfect plan.

3. Comment on the statement in this chapter: "Prayer is not a way for us to get God's attention! On the contrary, prayer is a way for God to get *our* attention."

Off the Main Trail

 There is an expression, "There are no atheists in foxholes." When we are in fear for our lives, we turn to God in prayer. It may be just as true in operating rooms and during tax audits! *Comment on what this need to pray when the chips are really down says about the human condition.*

Stepping-Stone

Here's a habit you can start cultivating this week. In fact, it's one to keep for the rest of your life. Every time you feel you have to pray for a specific need, STOP! Set the need aside and consciously open yourself to more of an awareness of God. Let any specific need be a warning flag, and bless it for reminding you of your desire to know God.

God lives in me as me.

Chapter Four

The issue everyone
has about prayer.

"But My Prayer Wasn't Answered"

> "I know that you can do all things, and
>   that no purpose of yours can be thwarted."
> —Job 42:2

"Help! My prayer wasn't answered."

Yes, it was,—our prayers are *always* answered. Now hold on . . . hold on! We know that statement might seem "Pollyannaish" and a contradiction of your own prayer experiences, but the statement happens to be true: our prayers are *always* answered.

"That's easy for you to say, but I know it wasn't answered because obviously I didn't get what I was praying for!"

Let's go back to our definition of prayer as being a sincere endeavor to experience the presence of God. If we can hold to that desire to know God more intimately and can surrender ourselves to the flow of Spirit in all areas of our lives, the divine plan best for us will be able to unfold. And the divine plan can be utterly trusted to bring about the very best for us. Where we often get into trouble is in trying to force our own human plans to develop. No matter how spiritual we might be, our human view is always limited since we cannot see from the more cosmic perspective. When we walk through a maze, all we can see is what is immediately in front of us. There is no overview. The best way out of a maze is to have someone viewing it from above tell you which ways to turn. What *we* see as best for us cannot possibly compare to what Spirit is trying to create for us.

If our prayers consist of putting in a request to God for some specific thing to happen—and happen exactly when, where, and how *we* think it should—we are setting ourselves up for probable disappointment. Prayer is not about judging a situation "good" or "bad" from our human perspective, then using our logic and intellect and energy to concoct a solution, and finally trying to enlist God's aid to bring it about. No, that is not the purpose of prayer. There is no coercive element to prayer. Our human manipulations and contrivances are not what prayer is about, and so any attempts at "praying" this way are apt not to be "answered." Prayer and God are infinitely more powerful than our individual human attempts to bring order to our lives.

Remember When?

How about those times when we prayed for some specific thing, only to be relieved when it did *not* happen! All of us can look back on our lives and see how, despite our disappointment at the time, we were actually grateful that things turned out differently from what we "prayed for." How many times have we been delighted with the way events unfolded in spite of our prayers, and how "right" they seemed when viewed from the broader perspective of time?

One wonders why it is so difficult to let go of the human will when what God wants to create for us is so opulent, so lavish, so unimaginable—in a phrase, *outrageously fabulous*! After so many years of remarking, "Ah, *now* I see why that happened," you would think the human race would learn to trust God a little more. It's something we're all working on, however, and we can help each other every time we allow ourselves to be lifted and guided by Spirit. In the meantime, until we're all living a life of absolute surrender to Spirit, we are learning and growing and experiencing more and more of the presence of God.

In a Nutshell

To recap, we pray to feel the loving presence of our Creator. Once we experience that presence, we are lifted into a sense of joy and peace. We let go of our human "wish lists" and allow Spirit to have Its way with us. The result of trusting Spirit in our lives? A flood of incredible blessings beyond what we ever could have imagined or asked for.

Put even more simply, we pray to become more "awake" to God. This opens us to the divine plan and thus "the word is made flesh." And . . . God's plan is *always* the right one for each of us. With that, our prayer is answered.

So let us pray, let us trust, let us open ourselves and wait for the Great Spirit of the universe to move through us in new and excellent ways. *This* is our true prayer. This is the prayer that is always "answered."

Mile Markers

- The divine plan can be utterly trusted to bring about the very best for us.
- There is no coercive element to prayer.
- Our human view is always limited and cannot possibly compare to what Spirit is trying to create.
- Once we experience the Presence, we let go of our human "wish lists."
- True prayer is always "answered."

Thank You, sweet Spirit, for your infinite wisdom and loving ways. I open my heart to all You are. I see the beauty and the gentleness with which You live Your life through me, and I am so grateful for the wonders unfolding each day.

Adventure Four

"But My Prayer Wasn't Answered"

There is more light than can be
seen through the window.
          —Russian Proverb[18]

"She is everything I want. She can't break up with me now. If she does, I'll just die! Please God, make her stay with me, make her marry me. Please answer my prayers."

But she didn't stay with him, she married someone else and twenty-five years later, when they met again at their high school reunion, he was so happy his adolescent prayer had not been answered!

Many of us have experienced it—we pray for something we think we can't live without. The prayer is not "granted." But years later, looking at all the twists and turns our life has made, we are grateful that the prayer wasn't "answered." We may even find ourselves thanking God for not "answering" that prayer.

Hence the wisdom: "Be careful of what you pray for. You might just get it!"

Soul–Talk

God, I am open to Your *plan for my life.*

1. _____

2. _____

3. _____

Soul–Thoughts

1. Recall a time or two in your life when you prayed hard for something and did not get it. Explain how it is clear now that what you had prayed for was not at all in your best interest.

Sometimes we pray out of habit. We feel we want something, it is slow in coming, and so we begin to pray. But specific prayers are directed only to specific results. It's like looking exclusively for silver in a mine rich with gold veins. In our specific focus on what we are looking for, we are not open to all the other blessings that are really ours.

2. Examine some of the things you are praying for now. *What are the chances that your idea of exactly what you need may not be God's idea of what is best for you?* Discuss this.

3. It's been said that if you are going to pray, don't worry, and if you are going to worry, don't pray. *What are your thoughts on this?*

Off the Main Trail

Just about all of us know someone whom we feel, deep in our hearts, is praying for something "foolish." It could be a small child praying to fly to the moon or a teenager praying to marry a movie star or an adult praying earnestly to win the big lottery. *If you know someone praying for something "foolish," detail your reasons for feeling that his or her prayers are less meaningful than your own.*

Stepping-Stone

An old adage advises we should not have what we want, but rather want what we have. What in your present life are you glad you have? Set aside a few minutes every day this week to prayerfully give thanks for this great blessing. As you sit quietly, allow your senses to savor the blessing—feel it. After the prayer time, take these elated feelings into your daily activities.

I am open to God's plan for my life.

Chapter Five

There is a major hurdle
to leap if we really
intend to be of help.

Praying for Others

> May I be a lamp for those in darkness.
> —from the Bodhicaryavatara of Shantideva[19]

Most of us have found ourselves wanting to help someone else through prayer. This is understandable, for it is natural, since love and caring are built into our hearts, to want to help those who appear to be going through a difficult time in their lives. But how do we do this?

Let's circle back to our spiritual journey's base camp—the premise that it is the experience of God which is the *real* need of all people. (We will always return to this base camp, for there we strengthen our faith and obtain new "maps" that will provide direction for us.)

While things such as "being there" for others in whatever ways are appropriate can certainly be im-

portant, we are limited in the human level of help
we can give to others by our talents, our time, and
our finances. But there is a higher level we can step
up to. When living God-centered lives, our help is
unlimited because we lift others by our mere presence. We become that unwavering bulwark of faith—
the steady flame—which sees the sacred Light in
everyone and every circumstance, even the ones
which might be deemed needing "help." When we
live this way, we serve as blessings to everyone who
touches our lives. Praying for others, therefore, becomes a matter of releasing those people to the activity of God and continually strengthening our own
awareness of this activity in them.

Some "How-To" Ideas

First, let's recognize that when we feel the need
to pray for someone, the real need is not to change
this person, although it may seem that way. The
need is to change our own thinking—our own perspective—regarding the individual. (Trying to change
someone else is fruitless, as we have all discovered!)
This is our biggest hurdle if we really intend to be
of help. We have to recognize that each soul needs
to experience whatever it requires for its own en-
lightenment, its own growth. There's no way any of
us can possibly ever know the soul needs of another
person, no matter how close that person is to us. To

think that we can is not only presumptuous, it is downright controlling and manipulative—a violation of the sanctity of a human soul. It's easy to know this in theory, but when we see a loved one in physical or emotional pain, it is very difficult not to get drawn down into a negative state of fear and/or worry ourselves. But stay above it we must, if we do not want to become part of the problem. Worrying about another person, adding our own fears, only attaches our own negative energies to the situation, which can make it worse.

So we change our own attitude first and lift ourselves into the consciousness of seeing the presence of God in the person and situation. This means letting go of the person's problem—and even letting go again and again if it tries to overtake us. This is crucial to our being of help because we can only lift others to our own level. When someone is drowning *in* the water, it's easier to pull them out if we are in a boat floating *on* the water. Thus we can only help them by being on a higher level ourselves.

The Power of Love

One extremely powerful and effective way to begin to help another is to send loving thoughts, rather than thoughts of worry or concern. Thoughts are palpable. They are real. They are potent carriers of our personal messages. When they are combined with the most powerful force in the universe—love—we are able to help others infinitely more effectively than by just worrying along with them. The presence of love is a healing presence and provides an environment that allows the activity of God to flow in its natural way. Our own loving thoughts and emotions are dynamic agents for transformation and healing and should never be underestimated. It is a most important first step in supporting others.

If we have regular access to the individuals we wish to help, we are of most benefit to them through our example by helping them to see the presence of God in themselves and in their circumstances. This, again, sounds fine in theory. But when someone we care about is in a dire situation, it takes patience and persistence and *great* trust on our part to help this individual begin to get a sense that God is always present—*even in the midst of his or her challenge!* The tricky part is that this cannot take place until we ourselves have a sense that God is always present—*even in the midst of challenge.* (Let's face it, this is simple in theory but often most difficult in practice and requires our continual attention.)

What of the actual prayers themselves when we wish to help someone? Simple in concept, but here again it requires getting ourselves in "the right space." When we pray for a person, we pray not *to* God, but *from* a consciousness of God. In this consciousness, we see the wholeness and beauty and blessings already available to the person and we use our prayers to affirm and acknowledge and give thanks for this Truth about the situation. Any words we might speak from this elevated consciousness are therefore true "Spoken Words" because they originate from the divine power of us. When uttered by us in desiring to bless other people, the intention of these words is to release the God-power within those people.

The "Spoken Word of God" has nothing to do with trying to manipulate people and events or making something happen. These *true* Spoken Words are devoid of any ego or personal will, and are essentially a release of the power of God within us.

Lift Our Own Selves

To summarize then, praying for others is not to beg God to change them or their circumstances, but rather to lift our own selves and, from a higher perspective, to see the wholeness already there. Only from a higher level can we lift others. This is the method used by most spiritual healers in their work. We all can learn to use it, becoming greater blessings to the people in our world.

When it comes to helping others through prayer, each of us must ask, "Am I lighting a candle, or am I merely helping someone grope in the dark?"

Mile Markers

- Praying for others becomes a matter of lifting our own consciousness and releasing these people to the activity of God.

- The need is not to change the person; it is to change our own perspective.

- Our goal is to be able to see the presence of God in every person and situation.

- Our own loving thoughts and emotions are dynamic agents for transformation and healing.

- It is only when we are at a higher level that we can lift others.

O Great Spirit, recognizing Your sacred presence in all people fills my heart with joy and wonder. May the love I feel for all creation be a blessing to everyone I meet.

Adventure Five

Praying for Others

Even a small star shines in the darkness.
—Danish Proverb[20]

Sometimes we pray for others because we think we know what's best for them. Too often our prayers are plans that we present to God to be fulfilled. But we never can be sure we know what's best for another person. All we can know is that God knows best and that we can trust God's plan.

Many years ago we had friends who were going through an extremely painful divorce. Being fond of both parties, we prayed for them to get back together again or, at least, for the divorce to take place quickly so the healing could begin. But that was not to be. The divorce process dragged out until both parties were emotionally and financially drained. Today, however, each of them says the growth was worth the pain they had to endure. If *our* prayers had been answered, neither would have had the growth in spiritual awareness that they are so thankful for now.

Many recovering alcoholics say, "Thank God, I'm an alcoholic!" They feel this way because the Twelve Steps of Alcoholics Anonymous are spiritual steps that one must live each day if one is to continue in his or her recovery. These people are actually grateful for their addictions! It was the catalyst for growth that led them to a spiritual path.

A professional football coach admits he cried for days when his son was born with Down's syndrome. He had plans for raising a son who would be an athlete as fine as he had been. But now, eighteen years later, he calls the boy the single greatest blessing of his life because his son has taught and continues to teach him about unconditional love.

Soul-Talk

I release my loved ones to God's care.

1. _____

2. _____

3. _____

Soul-Thoughts

1. Praying for others as if we know what is best for them is a dangerous game that we all have played. Recall two or three times in your life when you thought you knew best for someone and were proven wrong.

2. *Is there someone whom you are praying for now that you are worried about? How can you change your prayers so that you are more supportive?*

A Real Bonus

There's nothing wrong with holding a special, loving thought for other people. This benefits us as much as it benefits them. In fact, in some ways even more so. Consider, for example, what happens when you wash your car with a hose. What gets clean first? The inside of the hose, of course, because the water must rush through the hose before it can clean the car. So it is when we hold loving thoughts for someone. As those loving thoughts rush through us, they bless us first. It's a win-win situation.

3. Sacred literature of all faiths recounts examples of healings done by someone to someone else. Jesus, Buddha, Muhammad are but a few who are reported to have healed others. *How do these healings fit with the philosophy that we should never interfere with another's spiritual journey?*

Off the Main Trail

 What do we do if a friend comes to us and asks for our help? What do we do if s/he asks us to pray with them?

Stepping-Stone

 Think of someone in your life right now whom you are having trouble loving. It could be a boss, a coworker, even someone you don't know who is in the news. Write a loving prayer in support of this person and pray it each morning and evening for one week.

I release my loved ones to God's care.

Chapter Six

A unified prayer group
creates a "group soul."

Group Prayer

> O God, let us be united; let us speak
>   in harmony; let our minds
>   apprehend alike;
> Common be our prayer, common the
>   end of our assembly;
> Common be our resolution; common
>   be our deliberation.
> Alike be our feelings; unified be our
>   hearts; common be our intentions;
>   perfect be our unity.
> —from the Rig Veda [21]

Thousands of Roman Catholics praying together in St. Peter's Square, a group of lamas sharing a silent meditation in the Himalayas, a handful of Friends in a tiny Quaker meeting house—no matter the size of the group, joining together in prayer with others is decidedly rewarding.

For most humans, linking hearts with those who share a spiritual path or share a common purpose just plain feels good! Group prayer has the potential to be a rich and memorable experience, extraordinarily powerful, and at the same time very precious.

Something "happens" when a group of people get together to pray. The feelings themselves may be indefinable, but they are real nevertheless, which is probably why people have been praying in groups since the dawn of humankind. Somehow, without being able to explain it, without being able to measure the power we are creating—knowing only that it feels right!—we come together to pray.

Eric Butterworth speaks of the enormous power in group prayer that, he says, is generated when people can let go of their egos and surrender to the group energy: "There can be a buildup of that energy to a dramatic point. . . . It can become a pool of light, which may be radiated out to include specific persons or general situations in the world." [22]

No matter what the size, a prayer group with a common interest or purpose creates something greater than the sum total of its members. A "group soul" emerges that can nurture each individual as well as be nurtured *by* each individual. Butterworth refers to this as the "power of the swarm."[23] This is a transcendent force that seems to take over the entire group and to redefine the group into a more lofty and God-centered family of seekers.

A "How-To"

Depending on the makeup of the group, collective prayer can take any form. We, the authors, have found the format suggested by Eric Butterworth in his landmark book *The Universe is Calling* to be especially practical and effective.

The process begins when the facilitator calls for stillness, and everyone is invited to make contact with his or her own inner divinity. After a certain period of this individual worship, the facilitator may ask everyone to join together as one soul. At this point the prayer energy generated can be directed to whatever people or situations are desired.

The important thing to remember is that neither the group nor any individual in the group is praying *to* God. Rather, both individually and in concert, they are praying *from* the presence of God within. Each individual opens him/herself to the divine flow, and then *as a group* they become focused on the power of God blessing those in the group as well as all the world. The difference between praying *to* God and praying *from* an awareness of the Presence within can be likened to a fireman's trying to put out a fire by asking the hydrant for water rather than hooking up to the hydrant.

Almost Indispensable

The George H. Gallup International Institute has determined that more than one-fourth of the people in the United States are currently part of a small prayer group. "The fruits of their experience are remarkable and exciting in terms of deepened faith, prayers being answered, relationships being healed, being better able to forgive themselves and others, and in terms of helping them serve people outside their groups."[24]

Chances are if you are reading this book, you may be part of some type of prayer community. Whether they are large or small, prayer groups benefit the individual participants as well as the world in general. All prayers "seed" the universe with positive power, which is there for any of us to draw upon when needed. And prayers generated by a focused group of people take on an enormous strength.

If, when we pray together, we realize our individual prayers are also the prayers of everyone in the group, it helps us to know our oneness and to establish a spiritual connection between us all. If group prayer does not create this experience, it is merely individual prayer in a group setting. While that in itself is beneficial, it deprives the individual of one of the most precious and singular experiences possible—the experience of dissolving the boundaries of self and merging with the One as it expresses through the "many." It is that exquisite mystical experience which theologian Martin Buber referred to as the "I-Thou" moment, when we are no longer able to determine where one of us leaves off and the other begins.

For anyone believing in the power of prayer and who prays with any regularity, the added joy and strength of praying in a group is almost indispensable.

Mile Markers

- Group prayer has the potential to be extraordinarily powerful and at the same time very precious.

- A prayer group creates a "group soul."

- The group prays not *to* God, but *from* the presence of God within.

- Prayers generated by a focused group of people take on an enormous power.

- If group prayer does not create an experience of oneness, it is merely individual prayer in a group setting.

Sacred Spirit of Life, I surrender myself to Your mighty presence as I link my heart with all other praying souls on this planet. Thank You for Your love and peace, infusing all people everywhere.

Adventure Six

Group Prayer

When we pray together, I feel something, I do
not know the exact words—whether you would
call it blessings, or grace—but in any case there
is a certain feeling that we can experience.
                              —The Dalai Lama[25]

The energy generated when a group of people
come together to pray is enormous. Research done
on group dynamics suggests that groups dedicated
to a cause have power far exceeding the total number
of individuals in that group. The findings indicate
that there is an intensity developed when people
get together for the same purpose—any purpose. In
other words, when everyone is on the same wavelength, it creates a coherent group energy that is
greater than the number of people in the group. The
word *coherent* refers to the fact that the entire group
is focused on one object, their energies not dissi-
pated in different directions as a group of random
individuals' energies would be. (A laser is an example of the power of coherent energy. Unlike a light
bulb, which disperses light in every direction, all the

laser's light is in phase, all going in one direction. This singular focus of energy gives the laser a prodigious amount of power.)

How Powerful Is It?

The "intensity" of a group of people who have gotten together with the same intentions at the same time is not measured by the sum of the number of people in the group, but by the *square* of the number of people in the group! And so the intensity of 3 people who have formed a coherent group-energy is not 3, but 3 *squared*, which is 9. The power of 10 people forming a coherent group-energy field is not 10 but 10 *times* 10, or 100.

At an intuitive level, this really makes a great deal of sense. Think of it. Ten people who are connected in their thinking—who are on the same wavelength regarding a certain subject, and who all have the same intentions and have come together to address that subject—are a much more powerful group, able to get much more done, than a random group of ten individuals each with his or her own agenda.

How does it work? Why does it work? Probably no one knows. Perhaps it's that each member of the group is able to keep the other excited. Perhaps it's because if one member of the group loses sight of the goal, others will redirect his or her gaze. Perhaps there's a subtle psychological shift which takes place when we know that others feel as passionately as *we* do about something and they support us. Whatever the reason, a coherent group is mega-powerful. And when the purpose of the group is as lofty as prayer, the entire group is raised to an even higher plateau.

Soul-Talk

I join my heart with all who pray.

1. _____

2. _____

3. _____

Soul-Thoughts

1. Describe your feelings when you pray with others. *Does it differ from when you pray alone? If so, how?*

2. Describe any situations and/or circumstances when you feel that group prayer is more effective than individual prayer.

3. *If you wanted to form a regular prayer group, whom would you ask to be in your group? Why?*

Note: If you form a prayer group, how will you get
everyone on the same wavelength? After all,
each person has his or her own reason to pray
and way of praying. Yet all that's required, really, is at least one committed individual—
especially if this person is strongly motivated
from his or her heart. This can draw the rest
of the group into that same level of consciousness, and thus a coherent group energy is
created.

> 4. *How can a group of individuals pray
> "from a consciousness of God"?*

Off the Main Trail

Attend a prayer session or join a prayer group that you would not ordinarily consider being a part of. Perhaps it would be one that is a different religious persuasion than you presently espouse. Allow yourself to contribute to the power of the group. Allow yourself to experience the energy of the group. Write a paragraph or two on how it felt, how it affected you, what you put into it, and what you got out of it.

Stepping-Stone

Become consciously aware of the dynamics present in any activity you are part of this week that involves more than yourself. In other words, actively analyze the dynamics of each group of people you are part of. Do your part to make each one better.

I join my heart with all who pray.

Chapter Seven

Whatever words help us
to feel our oneness with
God—these are prayers.

The Language of Prayer

> You have made us for yourself,
> and our hearts are restless,
> until they rest in you.
> —Saint Augustine [26]

Throughout all time, our arid souls have expressed their unremitting thirst to know God. The great religions of the world all have had their prayers. Here are a few of them:

"Our Father who art in heaven,
Hallowed be thy name.
Thy kingdom come,
Thy will be done,
On earth as it is in heaven.
Give us this day our daily bread;
And forgive us our debts,

101

As we also have forgiven our debtors;
And lead us not into temptation,
But deliver us from evil."

                            —Christianity[27]

Heaven and earth, O Lord, are the work of
Your hands. The roaring seas and the life within
them issue forth from Your creative will. The
universe is one vast wonder proclaiming Your
wisdom and singing Your greatness . . . . O God
of life, the whole universe is Your dwelling-
place, all being a hymn to Your glory.

                              —Judaism [28]

In the awareness of God, the Infinitely Good,
     the Most Gracious
Perfect praise belongs to God, the Lord of all
     the worlds,
The Most Compassionate, the Most Merciful,
The "Lord of the Day of Awakening,"
Oh Holy One, you alone do I worship;
     and to you alone do I turn for help.
Please guide me along the right way of thinking,
The Way of thinking that leads to your
     blessings,

the way of thinking that does not
        incur your displeasure,
the way of thinking that does not
        go astray.

—Islam[29]

Supreme Lord! Lord of warmth and light,
Of life and consciousness, that knows all,
Guide us by the right path to happiness,
And give us strength and will to war against
The sins that rage in us and lead us astray.
We bow in reverence and prayer to Thee.

—Hinduism[30]

May no one who encounters me
ever have an insignificant contact.
May the mere fact of our meeting
contribute to the fulfillment of their wishes.
May I be a protector of the helpless,
a guide to those travelling the path,
a boat to those wishing to cross over,
or a bridge or a raft.
May I be a lamp for those in darkness,
a home for the homeless,
and a servant to the world.

—Buddhism[31]

The diverse cultures of our planet also have their own prayers. Here are some examples:

> Grandfather,
> Look at our brokenness.
> We know that in all creation
> Only the human family
> Has strayed from the Sacred Way.
> We know that we are the ones
> Who are divided
> And we are the ones
> Who must come back together
> To walk in the Sacred Way.
> Grandfather,
> Sacred One,
> Teach us love, compassion, and honor
> That we may heal the Earth
> And heal each other.
>
> —Ojibway prayer[32]

Today I will walk out, today everything evil will leave me, I will be as I was before. I will have a cool breeze over me, I will travel with a light body. I will be happy forever, nothing will hinder me. I walk with beauty before me, I walk with beauty behind me, I walk with

beauty above me, I walk with beauty all around me, my words will be beautiful.
—Navajo prayer[33]

Deep peace of the running wave to you,
Deep peace of the quiet earth to you,
Deep peace of the flowing air to you,
Deep peace of the shining star to you.
—Gaelic blessing[34]

Grandfather, Great Father, let matters go well with me, for I am going into the forest.
—Bambuti Pygmy prayer[35]

Bless to me, O God, the earth beneath my feet,
Bless to me, O God, the path whereon I go,
Bless to me, O God, the people whom I meet,
Today, tonight and tomorrow.
—Celtic blessing[36]

Dear God, be good to me. The sea is so wide, and my boat is so small.
—Breton fisherman's prayer[37]

Individuals often create prayers for themselves that others adopt and find strength and comfort in. Here are a few:

> Here, Lord, is my life. I place it on the altar today. Use it as you will.
>
> —Albert Schweitzer[38]

> Lord, make me according to thy heart.
>
> —Brother Lawrence[39]

> Lord, make me an instrument of your peace.
> Where there is hatred, let me sow love,
> Where there is injury, pardon
> Where there is doubt, faith,
> Where there is despair, hope,
> Where there is darkness, light,
> Where there is sadness, joy.
>
> —Saint Francis of Assisi[40]

> The light of God surrounds us;
> The love of God enfolds us;
> The power of God protects us;

The presence of God watches over us.
Wherever we are, God is!
                        —James Dillet Freeman[41]

May all beings be happy
May all beings be free from suffering
May all beings be at peace.
                        —The Dalai Lama[42]

For as long as space endures,
And for as long as living beings remain,
Until then may I, too, abide
To dispel the misery of the world.
                        —The Dalai Lama[43]

The reservoir of prayers throughout the ages is
vast and deep. We have touched upon only a very
few. The point is that wherever there are people,
there are prayers—there no doubt always will
be. There will always be words to give voice to
the longings of the human heart—if not our own
words, those of someone else. In our darkest
hours, we reach out in prayer and discover we are
not alone.

As the moon sinks on the mountain-edge
The fisherman's lights flicker
Far out on the dark wide sea.
When we think that we alone
Are steering our ships at midnight,
We hear the splash of oars
Far beyond us.

                              —Judaic prayer[44]

Mile Markers

- People crave ways to express their thirst for God.
- Virtually all religions and cultures of this planet have prayers.
- When we reach out in prayer, we discover we are not alone.

Divine Creator, the mystery of Your ways fills my heart with awe and humbleness. I see the beauty of Your presence everywhere and dedicate my life to acknowledging the sacredness of all creation.

Adventure Seven

The Language of Prayer

It is not well for a man to pray
cream and live skim milk.
—Henry Ward Beecher[45]

In light of the beautiful and meaningful prayers
from so many different religions and cultures, isn't
it obvious that *what* we say is not as important as
the state of consciousness in which it is said?
Whether we say "God," or "Dieu," or "Allah," or
"Dei," we are still referring to the Power that reigns
supreme in the universe and in us. Yet language—
how we phrase our feelings about this Power we
call God, the words we use, the emphasis we bring
to our words—is important because it affects our
feeling nature. Since we cannot intellectualize God
and since we cannot ever fully understand God,
then our feelings are the only vehicles by which our
understanding of God is given expression.

Soul-Talk

I am listening, God.

1. _____

2. _____

3. _____

Soul-Thoughts

1. Of the prayers presented in this chapter, which is your favorite? Why? How does it speak to you?

2. Which do you like the least? Why?

While people may use prayers written by others, we each are certainly capable of expressing ourselves to God in a very personal way. Often we do this spontaneously. For instance, we may ask God's help while our car is skidding on ice or if we have received bad news. Other than spontaneous outbursts of petitioning prayers, when is the last time you wrote out a prayer that truly expressed your feelings toward God?

3. Create a prayer that expresses your present relationship with God.

4. Just to show the contrast, write a prayer—original or one you recall—that expresses your relationship with God when you were a child.

5. *How do the two compare?*

Off the Main Trail

 Analyze the prayers in the chapter. What do all of these prayers have in common? What does this tell you about humankind's feelings and thoughts about God?

Stepping-Stone

 Select a different prayer for each day of this week and use it at least three times every day—especially in the morning and when you retire at night. Share your daily prayer with someone.

I am listening to God.

Chapter Eight

You can participate
in a divine mandate!

An Invitation—
The Next Step

> May all beings experience from
> one another
> The friendship of the heart.
> —from the prayer of a Hindu poet-saint [46]

Our world has become a global village. Through the wizardry of modern technology, especially television, telephone, and Internet, we can be instantaneously in touch with people on every continent. The age of unity is presenting itself to us, knocking at the door of every heart and demanding to be invited in.

With almost no deliberate action on the part of humanity, Spirit appears to be bringing about a global community of people who pray. As the former directors of Silent Unity, a worldwide prayer ministry serving people of all faiths, we have witnessed a rapidly expanding international body of people who believe in prayer and who are willing to be the agents through which Spirit can unfold Its plan for the world. These people belong to various religions as well as to no religions, for religion is not the criterion through which Spirit works. What we are speaking of goes beyond religion—to the spiritual essence within all of us—and it is here, at the heart of each of us, where we connect.

A Community of Pray-ers

People *want* to connect with each other on a spiritual level. Sharing a spiritual link with others is comforting, it is inspiring, and it fills the soul with new hope. The overwhelming response to events like Unity's annual World Day of Prayer, which experiences huge growth in participation year after year, continues to offer proof of this. When we were directly involved in Silent Unity, we were daily apprised of this, as more and more individuals as well as groups told us of their desire to feel part of this global community of praying people.

The idea of a worldwide community of pray-ers is being perceived by many among us, such as Richard J. Foster, who writes in his book *Prayer: Finding the Heart's True Home,* "I believe that God is gathering just such a community in our day . . . not only imminent on the horizon but already coming to birth in our midst."[47]

Henri J. M. Nouwen describes spiritual community as "the place where we keep the flame alive among us and take it seriously, so that it can grow and become stronger in us. In this way we can live with courage, trusting that there is a spiritual power in us that allows us to live in this world without being seduced constantly by despair. That is how we dare to say that God is a God of love even when we see hatred all around us. That is why we can claim that God is a God of life even when we see death and destruction and agony all around us. We say it together. We affirm it in each other."[48]

Divine Mandate

How can we possibly estimate the impact that a sizable community of praying people will have upon the world? When there are enough individuals whose lives are transformed by prayer, they can bring about a transformed, spiritualized "global village." This is not only an exciting and appealing concept—it is a divine mandate! Jeffrey Moses, in his little book *Oneness*, speaks in support of the need for our responding to this mandate: "The fullest expression of the Divine is found in loving relationships between people. Love is nourished by kindness, by concern for others, by forgiving, by sharing, and by caring for all of God's creatures. . . . Every act of good, no matter how small, helps radiate the Divine throughout the world."[49]

Can you sense it? Can you sense the movement of Spirit as It enlists more and more people the world over into a unity of caring souls—into a unity of prayer and spiritual purpose? Are you aware of how frequently the word *unity* is being voiced these days on the world scene? It is our nature to seek the community and the comfort and the strength of one another. Spirit, living Its life as each of us, is pushing toward the global realization and acceptance that there is only One. Do you see how perfect the name *Unity* really is? In the words of James Dillet Freeman, "Unity binds us not with vows and creeds but in a silent soul communion in a community of hearts. Perhaps it is in its name that the true meaning and purpose of Unity in the world is best revealed: Unity."[50] The age when Unity is to fulfill its name is here!

An Invitation

We invite you to join the rapidly emerging global community of pray-ers. We invite you to participate in prayer, no matter where you are or how you pray. It is the intention and the act itself that count. Begin to feel the stirring everywhere across this planet—

the stirring of souls responding to the call of Spirit. Let us pray daily, for as the Swiss theologian Karl Barth asserted, "to clasp the hands in prayer is the beginning of an uprising against the disorder of the world."[51]

The world needs praying people—people who recognize the presence of God in all persons and situations. There are no membership fees, no dues, no references required to become part of this new community of pray-ers. The only requirement is the commitment to prayer in our own hearts. Our prayers will move out from our hearts to encircle Earth with a mantle of compassion, kindness, and peace.

Mile Markers

- The world has become a global village.
- People *want* to connect with each other on a spiritual level.
- Spirit is drawing together a world community of people who pray.
- A spiritualized "global village" is a divine mandate.
- The world needs prayers.

Divine Creator, our eyes are open to Your presence, our spirits are alive to Your power, our hearts are united in serving You.

Adventure Eight

An Invitation–The Next Step

> In that which we share, let us see the common
> prayer of humanity. In that in which we differ,
> let us wonder at the freedom of humankind.
> —Jewish prayer[52]

There is something special about being part of a group—part of a community. The need to belong to an extended family has been in our genes for thousands of years. It has enabled us to build great cities, explore space, form great religions. Yet this need to belong is a double-edged sword, for it has also enabled us to engage in world wars.

Such is the power of a community of like-minded people. Whether it is sitting with thousands of others cheering your favorite football team or meeting with a few friends to share a love of certain music, being with others who are on the same "path" as you are is special. An "expanded soul" is formed that, although it cannot be explained or defined, is felt nonetheless.

This expanded soul is never stronger than when we pray with others, regardless of whether they are physically with us when we pray. Just knowing that others share our goal—our desire for more of an awareness of God—is enough to turn up the fire of our involvement.

Soul-Talk

I join in prayer with the worldwide community of pray-ers.

1. _____

2. _____

3. _____

Soul-Thoughts

1. Write a paragraph describing your feelings when you were part of the crowd cheering your high school team or some other happy event you shared with a group.

2. Do you do anything now that brings back at least some of those feelings? Describe it.

3. Describe your thoughts and feelings about being part of the worldwide community of praying people.

4. "When there are enough individuals whose lives are transformed by prayer, they can bring about a transformed, spiritualized 'global village.'" *What does this mean to you?*

Off the Main Trail

Take some time to sit alone in silence each day this week, and use your power of imagination to consciously embrace everyone in the world in prayer. Suspend all thoughts of other religious beliefs or ways of life, and connect heart to heart, soul to soul, spirit to spirit, with all who are on this Earth.

Stepping-Stone

We said that you can share your prayers with a group even if that group may not be physically present with you. This week, in your heart, become part of the prayer ministry of Silent Unity at Unity Village.[53] This century-old prayer ministry prays around the clock with people of all faiths and receives millions of calls and letters each year from people asking for prayer. When you pray this week, consciously become a part of this reservoir of prayer.

*I join in prayer with the worldwide
community of pray-ers.*

Future Quest:

Bearing the Torch—
A Final Thought

Prayer is a holy time within our hearts—a time of worship, joy, and thanksgiving deep inside ourselves. It is a time of lying down in green pastures, being led beside still waters, and having our souls restored. We come away from prayer renewed in body and mind and at peace with ourselves and our world.

The prayers we pray go forth like flares shot up into the night sky. The world needs light . . . we need light. Let us take time to pray, for it is the highest blessing we can give ourselves and others.

Blessings to you as you continue on your eternal Quest! It has been a privilege to share this segment of the journey with you.

Prayers You May Want to Pray

"Thank You, God, for Your ever-present
   sanctuary of love and joy and peace within
   my heart. My only need is to savor Your sweet
   presence in my life. I trust—truly trust—that
   I am in Your care and that all is well.
   Thank You, God."

"Thank You, God, for Your living Truth as it
speaks to me in unmistakable ways. I still
my body. I still my mind. I relax completely.
I surrender myself to You, God. Your presence
fills me as I wait in silence."

"Holy Presence within me, I am willing to
release all feelings of hurt and anger and
resentment. Help me know true forgiveness
and see each person as part of You. May my
words and my actions serve only to glorify
You. May they heal and comfort and
harmonize my life and the lives of
those around me. Thank You, God."

"Great Spirit of this universe, how glorious
are Your ways. My human mind cannot fully
grasp the magnitude of all You are, yet I know
I am Yours. Thank You for the safety of Your
guiding Presence—wherever I am, whatever
I do."

"Thank You, God, for the growing awareness
of who I am. You have created me to express
You. I make the commitment today to be Your

hands, Your voice, Your heart. Live Your life through me—fully and completely."

"The cells of my body shout for joy as they resurrect into new life! Thank You, God, for Your powerful healing presence as it touches every atom of my body, calling forth a radiant wholeness."

"I choose this day to serve You, God—to let my love radiate to all people and to be an inspiration to help lift others. My only prayer is to know You. Aware of Your sacred presence within me—as me—I am a blessing to all whose lives I touch."

"Gentle Spirit, I have heard Your call. I feel You drawing me closer to the realization of Your presence in my life. I hunger to know You more. I want to love You more and serve You more. I am willing to let You take charge of my life. Show me Your way, God, for I am ready!"

Suggested Reading

The Universe is Calling: Opening to the Divine Through Prayer by Eric Butterworth, Harper-Collins, New York, 1993.

An Easy Guide to Meditation by Roy Eugene Davis, CSA Press, Lakemont, Ga., 1978.

Healing Words: The Power of Prayer and the Practice of Medicine by Larry Dossey, M.D., Harper-Collins, New York, 1993.

Gates of Prayer: The New Union Prayerbook, Central Conference of American Rabbis, New York, 1975.

Prayer Works: True Stories of Answered Prayer by Rosemary Ellen Guiley, Unity Books, Unity Village, Mo., 1998.

The Quest: A Journey of Spiritual Rediscovery by Mary-Alice and Richard Jafolla, Unity Books, Unity Village, Mo., 1993.

Adventures on the Quest by Mary-Alice and Richard Jafolla, Unity Books, Unity Village, Mo., 1993.

The Gift of Prayer: A Treasury of Personal Prayer From the World's Spiritual Traditions, Jared T. Kieling, editor, The Continuum Publishing Co., New York, 1995.

The Path of Waiting by Henri J. Nouwen, Crossroad Publishing Co., New York, 1994.

Varieties of Prayer: A Survey Report by Margaret M. Poloma & George H. Gallup, Jr., Trinity Press International, Harrisburg, Pa., 1991.

A Closer Walk With God by Jim Rosemergy, Acropolis Books, Lakewood, Colo., 1991.

Living the Mystical Life Today by Jim Rosemergy, Inner Journey, Lee's Summit Mo., 1987.

Endnotes

1. "Hasidic prayer," *Darshan* magazine, January 1989, p. 24.

2. Loren Eiseley, *The Immense Journey*, (New York: Vintage Books, 1957), p. 44.

3. Ibid., p. 140.

4. *The Gift of Prayer*, compiled and edited by Jared T. Kieling, (New York: The Continuum Publishing Co., 1995), p. 171.

5. *Gates of Prayer: The New Union Prayerbook*, (New York: Central Conference of American Rabbis, 1975), p. 8.

6. Eric Butterworth, *The Universe Is Calling*, (New York: HarperCollins, 1993), p. 141.

7. Margaret Poloma & George Gallup, *Varieties of Prayer*, (Harrisburg, Pennsylvania: Trinity Press International, 1991), p. ix.

8. Ibid., p. 62.

9. *Instant Quotation Dictionary*, compiled by Donald O. Bolander (New York: Dell Publishing, 1972), p. 235.

10. Charles Fillmore, *Prosperity*, (Unity Village: Unity Books, 1998), p. 91–92.

11. Anthony de Mello, S. J., *Taking Flight*, (New York: Doubleday, 1990), pp. 21–22.

12. Matthew 6:7–8.

13. Chandogya Upanishad, in *The Gift of Prayer*, p. 37.

14. *The Gift of Prayer*, p. 58.

15. Ibid., p. 70.
16. H. Emilie Cady, *Lessons in Truth*, (Unity Village: Unity Books, 1995), pp. 86–88.
17. *The Gift of Prayer*, p. 216.
18. *Webster's Treasury of Relevant Quotations*, (New York: Greenwich House, 1983), p. 402.
19. *The Gift of Prayer*, p. 161.
20. *Webster's Treasury of Relevant Quotations*, p. 541.
21. *The Gift of Prayer*, p. 177.
22. Butterworth, p. 146.
23. Ibid, p. 145.
24. Poloma & Gallup, pp. 133–4.
25. *The Dalai Lama: A Policy of Kindness*, compiled and edited by Sidney Piburn, (Ithaca, N.Y.: Snow Lion Publications, 1993), p. 54.
26. *The Gift of Prayer*, p. 93.
27. Matthew 6:9–13.
28. *Gates of Prayer*, p. 83.
29. Al-Fatiha, (The opening chapter of the Qur'an, translated from a Unity perspective).
30. Jeffrey Moses, *Oneness*, (New York: Fawcett Columbine, 1989), p. 119.
31. *The Gift of Prayer*, p. 161.
32. Ibid., p. 96.
33. Ibid., p. 108.
34. Ibid., p. 198.
35. Ibid., p. 205.
36. Ibid., p. 237.
37. Ibid., p. 204.

38. Ibid., p. 135.

39. Ibid., p. 135.

40. Ibid., p. 158.

41. James Dillet Freeman, *Prayer: The Master Key,* (Unity Village: Unity Books, 1989), p. 258.

42. *The Dalai Lama: A Policy of Kindness,* p. 121.

43. Ibid., p. 25.

44. *Gates of Prayer,* p. 672.

45. *Proverbs From Plymouth Pulpit (1887), The International Thesaurus of Quotations,* compiled by Rhoda Thomas Tripp, (New York: Harper & Row, 1987), p. 497.

46. Dnyanadeu's Benediction, *The Gift of Prayer,* p. 244.

47. Richard J. Foster, *Prayer,* (HarperSanFrancisco, 1992), p. 254.

48. Henri J. M. Nouwen, *The Path of Waiting,* (New York: Crossroad Publishing Co., 1995), pp. 26–7.

49. Moses, pp. 64–65.

50. James D. Freeman, "Life Is a Wonder," *Unity Magazine,* January 1996, p. 46.

51. *The Gift of Prayer,* p. 132.

52. Ibid., p. 179.

53. If you have prayer needs, write: Silent Unity, 1901 NW Blue Parkway, Unity Village, MO 64065-0001 or call: (816) 969-2000. On-line: www.silentunity.org

About the Authors

Mary-Alice and Richard Jafolla are ordained Unity ministers, living in Vero Beach, Florida. Former directors of Silent Unity, the international prayer ministry located at Unity Village, Missouri, from 1991 to 1997, they have actively served the Unity movement since 1979.

Prior to 1991 they coministered the Unity Center of Vero Beach; published *Lifelines,* a national wellness newsletter; and created and developed Steppingstones, a highly popular line of subliminal tapes. In addition, they owned a chain of health food stores in California, Alabama, and Texas.

Mary-Alice has been a college instructor with an M.A. in humanities and Richard a drug counselor with an M.S. in counseling psychology. Both were teachers at Life Therapy Institute in Palm Springs, California. They also founded Spirit of Life, Inc., a nonprofit spiritual and educational organization dedicated to all aspects of wellness.

Mary-Alice and Richard are the authors of the bestselling *Quest* books: *The Quest: A Journey of Spiritual Rediscovery* and *Adventures on the Quest* which are the foundation for the Continuing Quest series. They also wrote *Nourishing the Life Force,* now out of print, as well as the planner/journals *Quest '96, Quest '97,* and *Quest 2000.* Mary-Alice also wrote *The Simple Truth,* which has recently gone through a revision, and Richard wrote *Soul Surgery,* published by DeVorss, which has been a national best-seller. They are authors of numerous pamphlets, articles in national magazines, and several cassettes based on *The Quest.*

The Jafollas have been popular speakers as well, having conducted hundreds of lectures and seminars nationwide, focusing on the role of Spirit in healing.

Is something missing in your life? This insightful book can help!

The Quest for Meaning

Living a Life of Purpose

by Jim Rosemergy

If your quest for meaning in life has meandered like a winding river, this book will give you both the spiritual lessons and practical applications you need to help guide you on your search for Truth. It is the first volume of the Continuing Quest series, designed to be a compilation of helpful guides in your journey of spiritual discovery.

In *The Quest for Meaning,* Jim Rosemergy will help you look inside yourself to discover your purpose here on earth, add meaning to your life, and find fulfillment in everything you do. You will discover the missing piece you've been searching for—an awareness of God's presence. You then will achieve fulfillment by expressing God in all you do.

$9.95, softcover, 134 pp., ISBN 0-87159-222-3, #11

Your Life Can Forever Be Altered Through the Power of Prayer!

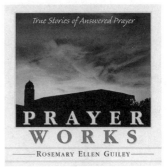

PRAYER WORKS

True Stories of
Answered Prayer

by Rosemary Ellen Guiley

"Prayer accomplishes many things . . . Through prayer, we attain an interpenetrating consciousness with God's perfect life and love and power."
—Rosemary Ellen Guiley

Prayer Works contains more than 150 true stories of human encounters with life's stressful situations and the divine answers delivered through prayer. In it are actual letters about life-and-death emergencies, broken and restored relationships, and miraculous healings. There are also stories about financial distress, depression, loss of self-esteem, and the distracting anxieties of daily life. In every case, prayer is the key to spiritual restoration and personal redemption.

$12.95, softcover, 192 pp., ISBN 0-87159-218-5, #5

A Guide and Workbook for Your Journey of Spiritual Rediscovery . . .

The Quest

Adventures on the Quest

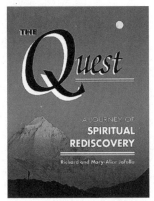

by Richard and Mary-Alice Jafolla

The Quest is a fresh, contemporary, and comprehensive presentation of spiritual principles that will lead you on a journey of spiritual rediscovery. Its companion, *Adventures on the Quest,* is a workbook that features suggested exercises and activities that will teach you to incorporate Christian principles into your life.

Written by popular Unity authors Mary-Alice and Richard Jafolla, these two best-selling books are now packaged as a set. Together they can make a powerful difference in your life.

The set: $24.95, softcover book, 410 pp., and softcover workbook, 375 pp., ISBN 0-87159-192-8, #15

Printed in the U.S.A.   82-0926-10M-9-99